The Wisdom of Oma

Dear Kelly,
With much love
and light,
Karen Braun

Karen Vos Braun

ISBN 1-894439-07-4
Printed and bound in Canada

For all inquiries, or to order additional copies of this book, please contact:

INNER Voice
Inner Voice
5-420 Erb Street W. Suite 434
Waterloo ON N2L 6K6
(519) 502-6047
www.innervoice.ca

Photos courtesy of Braun and Vos families
Cover image © PhotoDisc

Book design and production by
Baird O'Keefe Publishing Inc., *Publication Specialists*
  Wendy O'Keefe, Creative Director
  Gail Baird, Managing Editor

National Library of Canada Cataloguing In Publication

Vos Braun, Karen
  The wisdom of oma / Karen Vos Braun

ISBN 1-894439-07-4

1. Self-actualization (Psychology) I. Title.

BF632.V67 2002   158.1   C2002-902266-5

This book is dedicated with much love and thanks to my
Oma, Johanna Vos, and to all people who live with an open heart.

Only when the will of the personality and
the will of the soul come together evoked by love
does the soul dominate the material light of the personality.
—Alice Bailey

Acknowledgments

*I*t is with great appreciation that I wish to thank my family and friends (my created family on earth) for their consistent support and love given throughout all of my projects inspired by dreams and visions. With special thanks to my mother, Johanna Braun, for encouraging me right from the beginning and instilling the knowledge that anything is possible within me.

I am ever grateful to Robin Sharma for allowing me a mentor that truly lives the philosophies he speaks about.

Special thanks to...

- Alexis Barthelemy, for helping me connect my dreams to reality.
- Kathryn Braun, Shevaun Day Cressman and Judith Nicholson, for editing the first inspirations of this book and encouraging me to move forward.
- Gail Baird and Wendy O'Keefe, of Baird O'Keefe Publishing Inc., for embracing this book into their company and truly capturing the message within it.
- Shevaun Inc., for creating an awareness of the message in *The Wisdom of Oma* and for embracing my vision and allowing it to soar.

I wish to thank many of Oma's friends and mentors, especially Alida Bosshardt, for spending time, sharing and giving insight into their relationship with Johanna Vos.

It is with heartfelt appreciation that I thank this world and all those that roam within it. To the countless angels that have come in and out of my life, names unknown yet whose presence has assisted all that has come before now and everything that will occur in my future.

And to all of the healers on the planet seeking to provide more peace to our world.

'Thanks' is too limited a word for the appreciation, admiration and love that I feel towards Oma. Her daily vision of beauty in this world, despite the occurring events, will forever inspire me.

I also wish to thank all grandmothers who provide a space for children to grow and live where all of their dreams are possible and where they know they are safe and loved.

May happiness and fulfillment be with all those who read this book. Thank you for sharing the journey with me.

Contents

The Wisdom of Oma

There are moments that stay with us forever. Moments that when explained, are very brief in human time and yet amount to eternity in their effect over a life's journey.

A moment such as this, took place in a small hospital room on an ordinary day in March. A moment that became the greatest and most generous gift Oma could ever have bestowed. A moment when the world that is known and explicable crosses into a world which is inconceivable and unexplored. A moment that allowed a grandchild to walk the last mile of an extraordinary life's journey with her Oma.

This book has been written so that you the reader may enjoy the journey of insight and wisdom that only eighty-seven years can bestow. May your life be filled with blessings, light and moments similar to the ones that inspired this book.

Oma's first gift of advice:

*You can tell a lot about
a person by looking at their hands.*

Throughout Oma's life, Oma's hands were the center of strength to her life's purpose. In the early years of her life, while she was nursing during World War II, in Suriname during her years of mission service, and then in Canada where she worked and loved children with many forms of disabilities, Oma's hands were always an important part of her life's work.

Oma's life was dedicated to providing love and care to anyone who came in contact with her. Many times while growing up, I would fall asleep holding those hands, soft and strong from years of hanging wash on the line, cooking for anyone who walked through her door, caring and comforting those for whom society had no room, and raising a family of her own. While she was in the hospital for those final days and hours, many people would sit by her bedside in awe of her beautiful hands that lay resting. Hands that made everyone look at their own and wonder, 'what have we done with our hands, what have we given to this world, what can we give and who can we help?' Oma's advice has now become a challenge, a motivation to reflect and then to take action.

When you think about your own transformation from life to death, what will be remembered about your hands, your life, your impact on the world?

Everyday you have a chance to live as if you were walking hand in hand with the love and strength available to all of us for the asking. Every life has a purpose and meaning.

Oma's second gift of advice:

The "how" is not important, it is "what"
that is essential to living a life with purpose.

As you rise in the morning, ask yourself, 'what is my vision for today?' Be open to everyone and every situation that crosses your path. Understand that in some way, through your open receptiveness, there will be another life that breathes easier because you allowed yourself to express love fully through your actions.

Your work is to discover your work and
then with all your heart give yourself to it.
—Buddha

The key is to stop trying to tell your story and start living it. In the end, you can have pages of journals that express your dreams and desires, but until you start to live right now, in the present moment, your result will be only ink on paper—not a life well lived.

The irony of waiting for someone to announce your destiny is that no one ever will. It can be painful to realize that you are the only person responsible for your life and you are the only one who will be angered or hurt if you do not fulfill your life's journey. Take responsibility now and start living your purpose.

Oma leapt into every opportunity with the final answers unknown. Yet every leap of faith was answered by a solid landing. When Oma left for the jungle alone or when she accepted the first of many challenged children into her home, there was never a question of final outcomes but instead an acceptance of the present moment and an action that harmonized with her life's mission.

Witmarsum

Oma was born in this windmill on May 28, 1914. Windmills have become a symbol of the spirit of the Dutch people—a spirit that just doesn't acknowledge that seemingly impossible tasks, such as claiming land from the sea, may be too big for mere humans to tackle. I have always believed that it is somehow symbolic that Oma was born in one of these wonderful buildings.

Left: Oma in Groningen, a young woman with a life of adventures ahead.

Above: as a nursing student

Oma, third from right, and a group of young friends were excited that the war had finally ended. They are pictured here in costume after a night of celebrating their freedom with both Dutch and Canadians. (See page 78 for details.)

Oma arrives in Indonesia—ready, willing and able to continue on her path of caring for others.

The smiles say it all. Oma finds her soul mate, future husband Pieter Vos.

Oma's third gift of advice:

Anything is possible: you and I, without a doubt,
will accomplish great things in our lives.

Oma's life reflected and proved the philosophy that anything is possible and that anyone, no matter what their circumstances, can achieve great things.

The difficulty in the task is allowing yourself to accept life and live each day as it comes, trusting that God's plan is working for your highest good. Your responsibility is to *take responsibility* for your own life and allow yourself to remain open to your highest truth.

Oma's accomplishments are a testament to the truth that when one embraces, accepts and honors one's self-worth, only the extraordinary become the brushstrokes representing life.

Oma was known as "Mommy Vos" to hundreds of mentally and/or physically challenged children who knew no other mother but Oma. One particular child was born to a very young mother, who had decided to give up her baby for adoption before he was born. When the baby was born he had many unexpected difficulties and the adoption service could not find a home for him. So he was placed with the Children's Aid Society. The agency soon requested that Oma and Opa take this child into their care. Everyone assumed that the baby had Down's Syndrome because he was physically handicapped—his feet were clubbed, his knees were very weak and his head was bald. In the beginning, he would drag himself around; however, Oma soon realized that this child had a strong will and a great determination. Arrangements were made for corrective surgery and soon the child walked for the first time. Oma realized that the boy had been misdiagnosed and quickly moved him into her home and adopted him as another son. The young boy went on to complete high school and college, and graduated with an honors degree in counseling the mentally challenged. Oma and her family were there at every graduation and every success and stumble along the way. Throughout his life, this gentleman always came home to visit his mother, Oma.

You and I, from the time we were infants, were meant for greatness. There are always little signs, feelings and "wake-up calls" that come into our lives throughout childhood and into our adult years. Everyone has the opportunity to experience both difficult and easy times in their life. Every stage in life is linked together and each one is necessary. The opportunity lies in how you choose to embrace the particular stage you are in. When the questions lead to frustration, keep asking. Questions lead to answers about who you are and where you truly want to be. There are times when the questions will be answered through the actions you take in your life.

In times of smooth sailing, when the wind has caught your sail and the speed is ever increasing, don't get caught up with doubt or guilt. Embrace the experience. You have worked hard for this time of celebration — relax, take in as much as possible, and when the wind picks up speed, remember to have fun.

Oma's fourth gift of advice:

Let love be action in your daily life.

Oma could see the beauty in, and feel love for, people in so many different walks of life. Her willingness to act with love before anything else gives us a glimpse of the abundant wealth of love that is available for us to receive and express at all times and in all places of our lives.

> *If you judge people, you have no time to love them.*
> *And if you love people, you have no time to judge them.*
> —Mother Teresa

As a teacher in the classroom, I gaze back at eyes that are longing for love, belonging and acceptance. It takes so little effort to smile at the person who bags your groceries, to wish a good day to the person you see on the bus, or to call a friend to tell them you value their friendship. There is unbelievable power in the realization that we are responsible for living life with love in action.

Often in unsuspecting moments, despite any hardships you may carry, opportunities for joy and humor arise. In the beginning, when the home for challenged children was being established, new children were arriving weekly. Oma's eldest daughter would walk to school and on her way would pass the same police officer daily. Each day she would report that Oma had yet another new child. Well, one day this officer's curiosity grew and he decided to walk the little girl home. He knocked on the door and Oma answered. The police officer apologized for the surprise visit but explained that he just had to know if it was true that Oma had given birth to three children over the course of one week! Oma laughed and invited the officer into her home as she explained her new endeavor. Interspersed throughout the work of every day, there were always moments that created memories of joy.

It is important to see beauty in all of life and to learn to love yourself enough to express love for others. Upon stepping back and looking at the bigger picture, you soon realize that you don't need to be at an elevated level to express love and receive it. It can happen at any stage or in any state of mind.

Oma's fifth gift of advice:

Keep faith as your steadfast partner
on your journey through life.

Always keep a strong faith in yourself and in God, no matter what your circumstances are. Faith was Oma's steadfast friend and she practiced what she preached. Faith in action occurred when she hid Jewish patients in safety during the war. Faith in action occurred when she traveled alone into the jungle to establish the first medical clinic in Paramaribo. Faith in action occurred when she moved to a strange country with nothing but a strong belief that she was following her true path. And faith turned into action when she opened a hospital for children with varying degrees of disabilities at a time when these children had nowhere else to go.

Life has a purpose and meaning, so take control of that knowledge and do the best you can every day that you are given on this earth. Ask yourself right now as you read this book: what kind of person do I want to be? What do I want to be doing and what is my personal vision for myself? Have faith in the answers you receive and trust that if you live in truth you will discover that which is only for your highest good. In embracing the answers you receive, understand that flexibility is essential to letting go and letting God work in your life.

Stop! Take a deep breath! The most important person on this planet is you, never forget that. Live the truth of who you are.

Oma once talked about a dying soldier in his last moments, lying in a war hospital. This soldier called out to Oma, who was his nurse, and asked her to please come pray with him. The room was lined with other soldiers who were very "rough and grumble," and at first, Oma was apprehensive. But listening to her inner truth, she sat by the dying soldier's bed, ignored the other soldiers and prayed with him on the last night of his life here on earth. Imagine the peace that soldier felt as Oma held his hand and prayed with him as he expressed his last thoughts. A brief moment in human time and yet a moment that lasted forever in the hearts of Oma and the dying soldier. The effect of this moment went beyond Oma and the dying soldier to bring solace to those other soldiers who lay close by in their beds, not openly "seeking" comfort yet so in need of it.

Faith—in yourself and in your inner motivation—is essential. It is never too late to seed your own inner garden of faith. With little acts of love made every day, those seeds will grow into a beautiful garden of brilliant relationships in your life. Remember that every good gardener always cultivates patience for themselves and for those around them.

Oma was always filled with faith—the same faith that brought her through jungles alone, that raised six children and cared for hundreds more. Faith and hope are life's greatest gifts because in essence they are relief from any burdens you are carrying. They are promises that tomorrow and the day after will only get better. Faith and hope are the pathways that lead us home—the home that is our inner sanctuary where we seek solace and peace.

Never lose the faith that your life has meaning and purpose. Any great human who has ever walked the earth has had ample opportunity to stop evolving and think, 'who am I to achieve great things?' Faith held its course, as it will in your own life if you allow it to enter and take center stage. Anyone who lives and breathes can achieve heights greater and higher than they can ever fathom for themselves. The common belief is that only an exceptional few, blessed with rare and special gifts, can do great things. Take conscious moments during the day to remember that you too are exceptional. Express those rare gifts constantly.

Oma's sixth gift of advice:

What are you willing to give the
world so that they will remember you?
Ask yourself, what can I give?

I remember going to Oma's house for tea every week and sitting at her kitchen table pouring my heart out over the week's events. One afternoon I went over to her house and she had a guest visiting. The guest was discussing how overwhelmed and undervalued they felt at work. Oma always listened in a way that made you feel as if she really 'heard' what was being said. On this particular day, she smiled and responded, "Well, what are you willing to give the world so that the world will want to recognize you?"

Oma turned the issue around and showed the guest the other side of the mirror. If what we are doing is not contributing positively to fellow humans or to our planet, then how can we be recognized?

We are blessed with a mind that has the power to dream and choose, and the responsibility to use that power for the greatest good.

Dreams and choices do not come with limitations. If you have been blessed with a dream, you also have been blessed with the means to make that dream come true. Never let excuses or barriers hold you back.

Fame and recognition are not handed to people. Instead, fame and recognition are earned by cultivating the intention of bringing good to the planet and thus easing the plight of humanity in some way.

At times it is tempting to walk the path of another person's destiny. Perhaps their life seems "together" or maybe they have reached a financial or personal stage that is desirable. Instead, embrace the gifts you were given and run the path of your own destiny. Discover what dreams are actually your own and which ones belong to someone else.

This lesson can be a particularly difficult one to learn because much of our lives are spent trying to fulfill the expectations of others. From birth we are rewarded for "proper" learned behavior, and as we grow older we carry these lessons through school, at work and in our social circles.

Take the time to ask yourself if the people you surround yourself with, emulate the vision you have for your life and your goals for the future. Do your dreams, ambitions or current life titles have any relation to the top five things that bring you joy? If the answer is no, ask yourself why you are pursuing the things you are and who it might be pleasing. If the answer does not include yourself, you will find it impossible to reach your full potential because you are not living in harmony with your life's purpose.

Begin to release the false expectations you have placed on yourself, and open up your life to invite possibilities. Our own vision is so small compared to the vast vision of the universe. If the earth was made in the twinkling of an eye, imagine what that same eye could envision for your life if you were to trust its wisdom.

You are an exceptional human being and you are loved. Acknowledge and know that you are valuable.

Oma's seventh gift of advice:

Watch and engage carefully with the people around you.

Do those closest to you support who you are, where your dreams are leading you or the values and morals you live by? Do your friends value the essential you?

It is a known fact that the people closest to you directly impact and reflect who you are now and who you wish to become in the future.

Oma surrounded herself with the most interesting people from all walks of life. As a child I never knew who would drop in for coffee—a diplomat on vacation, a minister, an old-order Mennonite, local children or assorted other unique individuals. Each morning at ten o'clock, Oma and Opa would have coffee time. This entailed drinking coffee and eating something delicious. During the summer, I remember waiting by the door every morning at coffee time to see a little boy who would walk right into the house, and without saying a word, would help himself to a treat and a glass of chocolate milk and then leave. No one else seemed to notice this phenomenon. It was just another part of the day.

Oma's home was the world and everyone was welcome.

These experiences taught me about the interconnectedness of the world, and the beauty of those who bask in the light of their essential self. I learned to look for the wisdom they imparted, and the secret to the spark of light that shone in their eyes.

This was one of the great mysteries I endeavored to resolve when I stayed with Oma. I would look in her eyes, and the glimmer of light would be evident. With childlike curiosity, I turned to examine photographs, and sure enough, even the camera caught that same enchanting twinkle. I desperately wanted that sparkle in my own eyes and so sought to discover Oma's secret. I now understand that the twinkle is a gift that love, freely given through many years, brings to those who live with an open heart. When you choose to live in harmony with your personal path, the light you bring to the planet is so strong it beams from every vessel in your body.

There are times in every life when the loneliness of having a dream can be overbearing, when the people around you can be so far removed from who you are that it is impossible for them to support you on your journey. At these times of feeling different and separate from those around you, understand that their negative energy and lack of faith are their own issues. Know that to release them from your life is OK. Often as success unfolds in your life, you will experience a shift in close friends and family. Let go and let those individuals travel on their own journey. Having them nearby will only distract you from your own destiny.

Keep watch for people who seek to steal or dim the light that shines in you. When you accept yourself and grow to love your essential self, there will always be peers and colleagues who feel uncomfortable with your recognition of your own value. These distancing relationships are a part of the journey. By acknowledging the evolution of your essential self, you in turn allow your peers a glimpse into their own lives. This is a gift.

When there is something about someone else that makes you feel uncomfortable, the seed of the discomfort is usually the lesson ready to be addressed in our own lives. The issue of uneasiness does not rest with the other person; rather, it lies within you. By maintaining an awareness of your personal comfort zones, or boundaries, you allow yourself to build a firm sense of self-confidence. When you fail to honor yourself, you prevent your inner truth from expressing itself. As a result, personal boundaries are broken, creating space for shame and low self-esteem to take root.

Creating boundaries can be a difficult task. The transition point between what is unhealthy and self-destructive and what is healthy and positive can sometimes be difficult to discern. You may find yourself clinging to relationships that are holding you back from truly becoming the person you were meant to be. You may become limited by the boundaries another person has placed on your life. By releasing negative influences in your life, you are acknowledging your own self-love and understanding, and by doing so, you open up your life to receiving prosperity.

Oma's eighth gift of advice:

No matter where on the planet you roam, divine love always comforts and supports those who are willing to lay down their burdens and open their souls to the vibrations of the planet.

The essence of this advice derives from the old cliché that we are never alone. Open yourself to the possibility that love comes from many sources and not solely from fellow human beings. Everything is interconnected. When one human being shows compassion, this expression ripples out like a pebble hitting a calm lake, and embraces all living organisms.

How would your life be different if every minute you felt the love and support of the planet all around you? What would change in your life if you applied this new state of consciousness to your daily routine?

Oma's ninth gift of advice:

*All the day's worries can be soothed and erased
with a glass of honey water and a good night's rest.*

As a child when I couldn't sleep, Oma would give me a special drink of honey water. Despite knowing that Oma's water came from the tap and her honey from the same store I shop at now, I can never quite recreate the feeling I had as a child when I would hear my bedroom door open and see Oma carrying that delicious drink to my bedside. Oma's honey water somehow cleared away all my fears, which led to a restful sleep. As a child I thought of it as Oma's secret potion.

No worry is too big that it can't be tamed by a little soul tending. Perhaps your "honey water" is a journal, a piece of beautiful music, a spiritual passage, a picture or a meditation or affirmation that ensures rest for your body and mind. No problem should rob you of your personal happiness, health or ability to reach your maximum potential. You are not being selfish by releasing your troubles and sleeping with peace of mind. Instead, you are refueling your energy resources so that you can better serve the planet and the people who surround you. Allow yourself to maximize your talents. In neglecting to maximize your talents, you rob the world of what "could have been." In this respect, not reaching for your highest potential becomes a self-centered journey.

Oma's tenth gift of advice:

Enjoy the "bigness" of who you are.

Never try to keep your personality small or hidden. Enjoy the "bigness" of who you are. Express to everyone the beauty of your essential self.

One of my favorite anecdotes is one based on the truth about lobsters. The reason there is no lid on a lobster cage is that if a lobster attempts to crawl out, the others pull him back in. When we start to move forward, our uniqueness begins to shine through. Inevitably, many individuals react negatively, attempting to maintain old patterns. Still others may be too afraid to show their own light, choosing instead to ride along with your parade. Oma always maintained her individuality and stood straight and proud because she understood that her greatest asset and gift to the planet throughout her eighty-seven years was her own self. There is nothing more vibrant than someone who shines in their own light.

If you bring forth that which is within you, what you
bring forth will save you. If you do not bring forth what is
within you, what you do not bring forth will destroy you.
— Gospel of Thomas, Verse 70

In a time when everything in the media focuses on being small, **be big!** Give yourself permission to let go and enjoy the lush fullness of who you are.

Oma's eleventh gift of advice:

It's for the gezelligheid!

Whenever a guest entered Oma's home, they knew they were not just a visitor but a member of the household. Many tales of life and future plans were shared around the kitchen table. Of course, none of this occurred without Oma's famous cookie tins being opened. And, if anyone ever shook their head in refusal in order to maintain their diet, Oma would laugh, hand them the cookie tin and exclaim "it's for the gezelligheid!" (or "it's for comfort and companionship").

The gift that each visitor took home with them was the realization that the enjoyment of life leads to good health. There is a time for hard work and intense motivation, but in order to have balance in your life you must take time to stop and enjoy. Enjoy good food, music, company, your surroundings and even silence whenever that rare treat presents itself. Oma was right, no matter what burdens visitors arrived with, they were lightened by one hour's worth of talking and eating around Oma's kitchen table. Oma knew that through her giving she was also receiving.

Where you feel safe to experience love, you also are able to give love. Beyond the talking and eating, it was a very healing experience to sit in the presence of Oma and feel the energy of love and acceptance. We can create that environment in our own homes if we allow ourselves to open our hearts to all visitors who pass through our doorway.

The remarkable nature of Oma and Opa's home was that whether you came to stay or visit, life continued as always, and so the "guest" became a part of the household. Oma had many regular visitors because in her home they found a place where their essential self was honored. These visitors came from all parts of the world and shared extraordinary tales. Some visitors talked about the magic of the moon in their South Pacific homeland. Others discussed the sound of drumming echoing through the tall grass in a remote region of Africa. Still other visitors shared stories on the joy of sheep shearing in Australia. The stories were as diverse as the people who shared them. Without saying a word, Oma taught the importance of hospitality and how it wasn't only the guest who benefited but the host as well.

Take a moment now to breathe and look around. When was the last time you had fun? When was the last time you laughed uncontrollably? In what place do you feel accepted and loved?

It's funny how we work so hard to attain a comfortable life and yet may never take time to enjoy it. An annual two weeks of vacation time is not enough to create balance in your life. You need to include something every day that brings you pleasure and joy.

Joy can be found almost anywhere. One of the most powerful examples of this can be found in *The Diary of Anne Frank:* "We all live with the objective of being happy; our lives are all different…and yet the same." A young girl forced to live her days hidden with her family in an attic was able to create beauty and joy in her life and share love with those around her.

It is disquieting to think of the number of people who live in a home filled with everything they desire yet still do not experience moments of joy and hope. They drive a reliable vehicle, have employment with decent conditions and benefits, make enough money for food and entertainment, and still they are miserable. How is this possible when such stories as Anne Frank exist as blinding reminders of the gift of life itself?

The choices we make everyday and in every moment are what matter. Never give away the power to choose. While you can keep a physical body in captivity, you can never imprison the mind. The human spirit is a gift of wisdom in itself. **Are you consciously living?**

There is nothing selfish about living a life that shows you as you truly are. In times of struggle, hold fast to your inner core and know that you are strong enough to sail through the storm. Nothing is ever given to us that is too big for us to handle, solve or survive. Nothing of value comes without sacrifice. Be proud that you have been given an obstacle that will allow you to reach higher peaks in your life. Always remember that life is a cycle. Every low will be followed by a high. Be thankful for each period of change because it means your soul is evolving.

Where you are right now in your life is the perfect place.
Smile. Create an abundance of laugh lines!

Oma's twelfth gift of advice:

When circumstances arise that put you in a position of great anger, it is best to step away from the situation and breathe.

Anger is good. Never suppress anger in order to be liked by someone else. Find your own personal way of channeling anger into a positive energy. Try not to act while still in an angry and defensive mode. Step away and wait a few moments. Clear your mind of all the baggage you carry and define exactly what needs to be addressed and resolved in order to create peace with that person.

Understanding both sides to every disagreement is essential. The old adage "don't complain until you have walked a mile in the other man's shoes" is a reflection of this wisdom. Reach deep within and try to learn the lesson that arises from your feelings of anger. Each lesson is a gift that when cultivated can better your life.

In all the time I spent around Oma, I never heard her raise her voice, nor did I see anger rage across her face. Instead, she would turn possible angry moments into learning opportunities.

One day I was given the responsibility of collecting eggs from the chicken coop. I was told to be very careful because the eggs could easily break. I was able to collect all the eggs and was on the last nest when the mother hen jumped out at my head. I screamed, dropped the egg and ran for cover. After the shock passed and I realized I was still alive, the picture of the broken egg appeared in my head. I went inside and began sobbing while I explained the situation. Oma's eyes lit up; she laughed and told me that she herself had made plenty of mistakes and I shouldn't worry over this one. Oma always had a knack for turning what could be a tense situation into a humorous moment.

There is an ancient saying that instructs: You have no friends; you have no enemies; you have only teachers.

Anger is a natural response to many types of situations. If you don't ever *feel* angry, maybe you should ask yourself if you are truly honoring your essential self. Exercise, writing, music, silence, meditation and reading an affirmation are all great ways to channel anger energy into a positive fuel resource.

Being empowered is having the ability to step away when anger would otherwise surge through you. It is the ability to answer the confrontation with complete peace of mind and spirit, and to intuitively become aware of the anger buttons you carry and know when to shut them off.

He that wrestles with us strengthens our nerves, and sharpens our skill. Our antagonist is our helper.
—Edmund Burke (1729-97)

Oma's thirteenth gift of advice:

Give thanks for all the blessings that are in your life.

I believe that Oma's positive attitude allowed her to live a long, healthy and prosperous life. Every night, despite the troubles that may have occurred during the day, she would fold her hands over the dinner table and give thanks in prayer for all of the experiences during the day.

In every life, in every day, and in every moment, there is always something to be thankful for.

I asked God for all things that I might enjoy life.
God said, "No. I will give you life so that you may enjoy all things."
(author unknown)

I remembered those moments on one of the first days I had moved away from home to attend university. It had been a frustrating day of orientation and organization. I came home feeling exhausted and alone. I decided to make a list of the things in the day for which I was thankful. This is how it went:

I am thankful today for the beautiful weather, meeting a very interesting professor, for finding a beautiful space with a grand piano to practice in and for all of the wonderful, loving friends that I have and will meet this year. I remind myself that if I do what I always have done, I will receive what I always have received. I am thankful for the new adjustments I have to make in life because they will allow me to become a more conscious being on this earth.

As much as I felt that this list wouldn't change anything, by the time it was finished I felt a lot better and was ready to make new goals for the next day. Start your own list, and if you feel as though you can't think of anything, I have included an anonymous e-mail I received to assist you.

If you have never experienced the danger of battle, the loneliness of imprisonment, the agony of torture, or the pangs of starvation, you are ahead of 500 million people in the world.

If you can attend a church meeting without fear of harassment, arrest, torture, or death, you are more blessed than three billion people in the world.

If you have money in the bank, in your wallet, and spare change in a dish someplace, you are among the top eight per cent of the world's wealthy.

If you can read this message, you are more blessed than more than two billion people in the world who can't read at all.

I found this e-mail to be a personal wake-up call to be more thankful for everything I have in my life. Oma would always talk of her many adventurous travels; however, each story would end with how thankful she was to come home. I never fully appreciated home until I started traveling. The more I travel, the more I understand why Oma gave thanks for every day she lived in her home.

We have all we need to be happy. Happiness is about personal responsibility, not outside circumstances. Life is every minute of every day.

Set aside time every week to organize life's necessities. In this specific time you have scheduled for yourself, work through your bills, debts and any other financial responsibilities. Create a realistic plan and clearly understand your situation. Decide what action needs to be taken and write down any reminders you may need in your calendar. This concept is not only useful in finances but can be adapted to relationships, work and self-image issues.

How much time do you spend thinking about something without ever attempting to find a resolution? Naming your issue is the first step to resolving it.

When this organizing time is over, finish thinking about these items listed above and move on. Use your energy to further your own potential and goals.

Depression often begins with dead-end thoughts circling within your mind, clouding your view of the world. In time, you stop recognizing the blessings that exist in your life and see only a dark tunnel of self-doubt.

When I remember stories of Oma traveling on a ship crammed full of people with no space to breathe, or arriving at a farm that was falling apart and using her own clothes for insulation between the walls, I realize that Oma's life had its dark moments, as every life will. There is no human being who will escape sadness or loss.

Life is not always easy, nor will it be blissfully happy at all times. The key is to live the darker periods in life as though they were the brightest. Bring that open, energetic being with you into the darkness and learn all that you can. We are like all living things on the planet; in order to fully bloom we need night as well as day. We need both times to fully understand and tap into all facets of ourselves. Honor and give thanks for the painful times and always "live" through them. So many people decide when they see the clouds heading their way to go to sleep and hopefully awake when the storm has passed over. Unfortunately, you don't get to grade three by sleeping through grades one and two. Similarly, life doesn't get better if you don't embrace the lessons that come your way.

Imagine being alone in a small dark room, far from your home country. You are in your eighth month of pregnancy and you discover you also have malaria. How might you react?

Oma chose not to allow her mind to be controlled by her circumstances, and as a result her body released the disease in a remarkably short time. Oma returned to her life's work of helping people as soon as she was on her feet again.

Oma had a purpose and *chose* to live the dark and light periods of her life valiantly. To choose— that is the power each and every one of us has within us everyday. Who are we not to choose a life of purpose and thus happiness?

Embrace the idea that life will have difficult stages. The gift that is given during these times is self-revolutionary. You will walk out of the tunnel a more enriched and colorful person.

Before reading further, write down three areas of your life in which you would choose to live differently. When you finish, reflect on what you have written and think of ways you could begin incorporating these new ideas into your life. You have power over your life; take responsibility, grasp the reins and make it a fantastic journey.

If you have to paint the picture anyway, why not make it a masterpiece?

Oma's fourteenth gift of advice:

Always live your life with the intention of helping others.

Oma once said that her highest ambition was to help others who could not help themselves. She made this her goal during her teenage years. She realized that when you are not living with the intention of helping others, you will never reach your maximum fulfillment.

I don't know what your destiny will be, but one thing I
know: the only ones among you who will be truly happy are
those who will have sought and found how to serve.
—Albert Schweitzer (1875 – 1965)

Oma served others while nursing in Holland, Suriname and the jungle, and by establishing homes for children with disabilities. She embraced the word "service" in every moment of her life.

She describes a story of two boys who were brought into her hospital from a nearby prison camp during the war. Oma soon discovered that one of the boys had been engaged to be married just before Holland was occupied, and had not seen his fiancée since. This particular boy's fiancée had not been taken as a prisoner by the Nazi regime and lived close to the hospital. In order to give him a chance to see his sweetheart, Oma moved another patient who was not imprisoned by the Nazis into the room. Oma then contacted the boy's fiancée.

When the girl arrived at the hospital, Oma explained to the soldiers that the girl was visiting the new patient and not their prisoner. As a result the engaged couple were able to visit with each other.

Even in desperate situations, Oma created light wherever she went. Oma's life mission was to help those who could not help themselves, and in reflection one realizes how far she reached her hands to fully commit to her purpose.

Oma loved the jungle and made several discoveries about life and her self. She discovered that **trust was the most essential ingredient to healing.** This concept is true in every life: Trust in yourself and in the love around you. It is essential to have such trust before you can attempt to heal yourself and others.

Another discovery that Oma made while in the jungle was that **if you give yourself to your work, you become a real light and cannot help but love what you are doing.** The place in which you work does not determine whether you can bring light to it; *you* decide. Do you accept the idea that it is possible to love your work and that you deserve a life of fulfillment?

It is difficult to embrace a job that is in tune with your desires and talents when you cannot accept and love yourself. You will consistently get in the way of your own happiness. By dedicating your energy to one dream at a time and accomplishing your goals, you increase your self-confidence, drive and motivation and in turn, your prosperity.

> *Oh Man! There is no planet, sun or star could*
> *hold you, if you but knew what you are.*
> —Emerson

Embrace who you are at this moment. Let your inner light surge through you, expressing your essential self. Let no outside factor stop it. If you are basking in your inner light then your inner voice has a place to be heard.

Oma did not decide when and where it was appropriate to turn on her light. She was the light in every moment that she breathed. Because of this, she was an incredible success in business as well as nursing. You will prosper more financially, emotionally and physically by living in your own self-initiated light than by living in anyone else's.

There were many times that Oma could have taken the road already paved. She was offered excellent positions in fully equipped city hospitals, but she left that road and created her own. She answered her inner voice with a resounding and triumphant call. She answered this call by setting up

the first medical clinic in the jungle, hiding Jewish patients from Westeborg, praying with dying soldiers, running through streets that were lit by incoming bombs to nurse those who were injured, and
by traveling across the world to open hospitals and homes for disabled children who were not wanted
by their own parents. Oma's answer to her inner voice was her life in action.

What is your inner voice saying to you?

Declare your truth and listen to your inner voice.
—Shevaun Day Cressman

Happiness is a choice — may it be yours in this lifetime.

Oma's fifteenth gift of advice:

Lay your worries beside you, and move on.

When anyone talked to Oma about the disappointments in their life, she could often be heard telling them to put those thoughts "beside them" and move on. She believed that thinking and dwelling on the past limits our access to the abundance of prosperity that awaits us all.

You are not servicing the world by dampening your light. You are a beautiful, intelligent, gifted human being with a purpose; do not be selfish and waste the life you have been given. It is selfish to not take time for you. Let others experience the joy of who you are right now.

How do I know that you are an incredible human being? You are reading a book that falls under the subject of inspiration or self-help. You already have initiated the process of discovering yourself. You are alive, and every being that has life also has a purpose. I congratulate you for having the courage and motivation to live that purpose.

Another common limiting thought derives around the issue of money. Perhaps you feel that you could never be rich, or that by doing a particular activity or going to a certain school you are "out of your league." There is no league. Countless times I have been told that something was not possible due to financial realities, and countless times I have proven those voices wrong.

Imagine the year 1914. Women couldn't even vote, and yet Oma pursued a career in the medical profession. I am sure there were people who shook their heads in amusement and thought it could never happen. What they didn't realize was that while they were wasting their time thinking about someone else's dreams, those dreams were already becoming a reality.

The first step in initiating an action is naming it, the second step is believing in it, and the final step is doing it. It is not "luck," it is not money and isn't something special that is handed down to a few people. The trick to achieving your goals and dreams is hard work, perseverance and a lot of self-work. You have to know what you want in order to get it. You don't go the grocery store, stand outside and then leave with everything you need. Instead, you consider what groceries you need or want, you make time to drive to the store, enter, purchase the items you require and carry them to your car. That process is similar to what you need to do for your emotional well-being.

First, make time for yourself. Then foster the courage you need to delve inside yourself. With the information you derive from spending time in your inner world, you can then create a list of goals and future dreams. Finally, dedicate time and money to those things necessary for the achievement of your goals. As you accomplish successive goals, you bring knowledge and self-confidence to each new goal you envision. The dreams and goals are endless. They expand and get better with every success you create.

Write down three things that come to mind when you think of success. What would you need to do in order to have those three things in your life? Is it more education? A new community? Or do you need to overcome some personal barriers?

Oma never planned to have the success she did. However, she did plan to help those who could not help themselves.

You are the only person who knows what direction *feels* right. Answer that calling and ignore all the voices that say otherwise. Once you accomplish that particular goal, the road doesn't end; it only grows wider and longer. With every new step, life becomes more enticing and exciting.

In the movie *A Knight's Tale,* there is a young peasant boy who wants desperately to become a knight. One day he is attending a parade with his father and he proclaims this desire out loud. An old man nearby starts to laugh, and informs him that knighthood is for nobility and it is not in the boy's stars. The young boy, puzzled, looks up at his loving father and asks, "But father, can't one change their stars?"

This tale is set in the medieval times, yet sadly, society consistently passes down limiting beliefs to each new generation. You *can* change your circumstances with courage and self-understanding. It does not matter what your ancestry is, what your economic status is, or what gender you happen to be; your life is yours for the taking. How you choose to live is your responsibility.

Take a few moments to write down some of the thoughts that come to mind when you think about life in these terms. What limiting beliefs were you given as a child? How much of your current circumstances are truly self-created and how much derives from outside factors?

Life is ever changing. The person you are today could be completely transformed tomorrow. If you choose to deal with the issues that are preventing you from acting in a grounded and centered place, then you drastically change your stars, so to speak. Explore ways to create change in your life.

By making one conscious change in your personality, physical body or outside environment, you become the carver. You choose what to set in stone. How you choose to chisel your life sculpture depends on the answers you are willing to uncover.

Never let anyone rain on your parade. If advice feels wrong, walk away. Be your own mind's filter. Take the information that honors your highest good, and place the rest of the jargon beside you.

Everyone has intuitive abilities. The extent to which they are used is directly linked with how in tune you are with your essential self. Consider this: Have you ever picked up the phone and knew who it was going to be before you spoke? Have you ever called a friend who had been on your mind only to realize that your friend is in need or sick? Have you ever been singing a song in your head and turned on the radio only to hear the same song being played?

Your body is connected to your mind and your spirit. When these three areas function in harmony, you become very powerful.

Oma's sixteenth gift of advice:

When you ask, believe you will receive.

Remember to trust yourself because the fear that comes when you lack this trust will prevent you from finding and taking your true path. Know yourself, know your strengths and know your weaknesses. The greatest task we have in this life is to address the lessons we need to learn, admit we are not perfect, and turn our weaknesses into strengths.

Know that in the end you are the final player at bat. Will you look at your life and only make first base, or will you confidently hit a home run? Life is energy, and energy is always moving. Make sure that your energy is pushing you forward.

Take a few moments to begin a list of everything that you desire in life. Make your list a reflection of your dreams and goals. Make sure you return to that list now and again as a reminder of who you are and where you are going. Sometimes a reminder of our projected destination gives us enough steam to keep moving through difficult times. Make sure you are specific.

Has there been a time in your life when you knew exactly what you wanted but settled for something else because you felt inadequate or undeserving? Perhaps an item was too expensive for you to buy for yourself and yet the price seemed fine when you bought it for somebody else.

In order to get what you want, you first have to know what it is and then believe that you deserve it. Always honor yourself and only ask for your highest good.

And all things whatever you ask
in prayer, believing you will receive.
Matthew 21:22

Oma's seventeenth gift of advice:

As a human being, you have many facets.
Explore each one, and create a bouquet that
represents all of you, not just individual petals.

Oma was a jack of all trades and a master of many of them. Her actions unveiled many talents and attributes that she embraced and used throughout her life. Nurse, musician, missionary, mother, businesswoman, program coordinator, wife, sibling, grandmother, political activist and humanitarian…all were hats Oma wore equally well.

Growing up, I spent much time feeling frustrated while trying to figure out whether or not I was on the "right" path. Every decision I made was carefully examined and analyzed. It was a revelation for me to discover that there is no right or wrong choice. Instead, everything is part of the path, every minute of every day. You do not have to focus on one talent or one area of your personality, you can explore the multitude of possibilities that exist in each of us. With this realization comes the ability to let go…to grasp the courage to allow yourself to experience and trust all the moments that occur in your daily life.

When life is experienced without the limitations of constant attempts at control, suddenly the magic of every day becomes visible. You experience all of life's coincidences, and you begin to recognize soul friends and moments of perfection. Everyday living becomes very intricate and beautiful, and your sense of peace and happiness begin to soar.

Human life is like the phoenix, the mythical bird that triumphantly rose from the ashes. Each time you feel you are in the ashes and that all your bridges have been burned, take comfort in knowing that you will arise from those ashes a more exquisite and unique human being. Each time you arise, you offer the planet another gift—the gift of a closer look at the essential you. You cannot live your true purpose fully until you give your life to your own light.

Oma's eighteenth gift of advice:

*Love every living being and never prejudge
how much they can hear, see, taste or feel.*

A very touching story was told at Oma's funeral about a visitor who had come to her house. During the time when Oma and Opa were taking disabled children into their home, Oma had changed her living room to a nursing room for hydrocephalic babies. As these infants lay in their cribs, seemingly unaware of anything, the visitor asked Opa, "What is the point of caring for these deformed children? Do you really think they understand the difference?" Opa smiled and, with a twinkle in his eye, replied; "Watch as Oma passes through the room."

The two men waited quietly, observing as Oma made her way through the room. As she passed each crib, without being able to see her, each of the baby's eyes lit up with excitement. Little smiles formed on their young faces, showing the love they felt.

Oma left no one out. Her boundless love went beyond simply helping. She gave infants, children and adults alike a reason to smile and a reason to be thankful for life.

Life is not measured by the number of breaths we take,
but by the moments that take our breaths away.
(author unknown)

Conscious living happens when you are basking in your light, when you have shed the skins of other facades and are living who you are. It comes when you have taken time to work through your fears and desires and understand yourself at various levels. Finally, it enables you to understand the past, plan for the future, and most importantly, to live in full awareness of the present.

Oma's nineteenth gift of advice:

Everything on the planet is interconnected.
As Martin Luther King Jr. said,
"Injustice anywhere is a threat to justice everywhere."

Sometimes it is difficult to imagine that one small act of kindness can ripple into the lives of many people. Often the smallest acts create the biggest changes.

Whatever act you do for one, you do for all of mankind. There are countless documented reports recounting the benefit and the power of prayer and meditation. By giving love to one individual, you allow that person to give love to someone else. Like a ball, you send it rolling and the road it travels can be endless.

You are connected to the circle of life. Your breath and exhalation is shared by every living being on the planet. This ebb and flow is constant and unchanging. If unfairness is dealt out in one area of your nation, it is as if it is dealt out in your own home. When Oma embraced a disabled child left by a stranger, she also embraced you.

When you give of your time, money or resources, you in turn will receive more time, money and resources. When you embrace this concept and implement it in your life, you not only leave a legacy where you have walked but also anywhere that breath can travel.

> *The earth does not belong to man; man belongs*
> *to the earth. This we know. All things are connected like*
> *the blood which unites one family. All things are connected.*
> —Chief Seattle

I believe that because Oma supported and loved me unconditionally, I will live a life that supports my own experience. I believe that I am a small part of one of the many ripples cast out from the extraordinary life Oma gave to this planet. It is amazing when you realize the potential power everyone has at their hands to use at their will.

It is astonishing that in all the information thrown at us by various forms of media everyday, somehow some of the greatest daily miracles are missed. Within our own communities there are people living unbelievably giving lives, and we as fellow citizens aren't even aware of them. In doing research for this book, I came in contact with brilliant lives that are bringing much light to other lives both in the present and for future generations. Through my research, I was fortunate to have elderly people share stories and information about Oma and her history. Those visits made me realize how distant modern society has become from the aged population. As a result, much wisdom is being overlooked, or even worse, lost.

Another gift Oma shared through her life's example is the realization that it is not always necessary to reinvent the wheel. The innovators and inventors of everything that surrounds us are currently sitting alone in the aged homes of today. One only has to watch the movie *Fried Green Tomatoes* to feel the impact that the older generations can have on our lives. These people have so much wisdom and so many lessons to impart.

May our ancestors breathe blessing onto us for our
eyes to open, and our life purpose to become clear.
—Dagara Prayer

Oma's twentieth gift of advice:

Know who your heroes are.

An excellent exercise to explore while you are defining your life mission and translating your inner dialogues is to name your heroes. By heroes I mean the people you most aspire to be like for one reason or for many, people you feel "have arrived" at a place where they are basking in their inner light. By reviewing the qualities your list of heroes have in common, the essence of who and what you strive to be will become visible.

Oma had a hero of whom she spoke, whose name is Alida Bosshardt. Alida Bosshardt is from the city of Amsterdam in the Netherlands. An airline company has admired her so much that a plane has been named after her. The queen has noted her life's contribution by naming twelve tulip varieties after her.

Alida Bosshardt decided that her life's mission was on the streets of the red-light district of Amsterdam. Bosshardt was called at a young age to bring love and support to girls living as prostitutes.

At the beginning, Bosshardt was told that she was too weak and would never last doing that type of work. However, she is now in her eighties and still living in Amsterdam, still sharing her love when it is needed.

People who have met Bosshardt know that she is one who basks in her own inner light, one who sparks a fire in anyone lucky enough to be near her. She has traveled all over the world, both as a speaker and an honored guest. Her life has been used as an example for other missionaries, and is an inspiration for the general public in Holland. She has published 12 books that delve into the wisdom she has acquired from living life in the presence of the moment, and she willingly receives inspired guests who would like to share stories over a cup of tea.

When you meet with people who have become friends with Bosshardt, their eyes light up when you mention her name. Love and admiration spill forth as friends recount their time shared together.

Upon seeing the sparkle in Bosshardt's eyes, I looked to see what attributes she had in common with others who carried this light. The secret came back to the idea of fully living in your own inner light. People who shared time with Bosshardt or Oma know that neither of the two women accommodated the other's personality by dimming their own light to play hostess and guest.

If you spark the match to light talent, then it is in your hands. Is your flame going to flicker in the breeze and quickly disappear, or is your flame a fire blazing strong, reaching closer and closer to the limitless sky above?

Imagine your heroes as your angels or guides walking with you into the board presentation, accompanying you as you begin your own business or supporting you as you begin the process of discovering both the good and bad you are storing within your mind. All that they are, you are as well. Your dreams are bold and profound because they are yours. No one can live your life as well as you can.

Oma shared that message by living in her light. She knew that in order to support other people and allow them to express their individuality, she had to honor her own space as well. You are not selfish when you take time to get to know yourself. Instead, you are allowing yourself to fully make a contribution to your community. In return, you will leave an unforgettable legacy.

By becoming your essential self and living as that person, you give a gift to all the people who come in contact with you. Everything you do to heal yourself reflects outward, healing others.

You are a child of God. Your playing small does not serve the world. There is nothing enlightening about shrinking, so that other people won't feel insecure around you. We are born to make manifest the glory of God that is within us. It is not just in some of us; it is in everyone. And as we let our light shine, we unconsciously give other people permission to do the same. As we are liberated from our own fear, our presence automatically liberates others.

—Marianne Williamson

This is how Johanna and her fellow workers traveled from village to village in Indonesia.

Prayer and music were always important parts of Johanna's life.

Oma and my mom…I love this photo!

Oma and Opa come to Canada. Like all Europeans who come to live or visit, Niagara Falls was a must-see.

Pieter and Johanna remained soulmates throughout their life together. Sunbeam Home, shown at left, was one of the outward signs of their love for each other and those around them.

Johanna Vos.
My Oma.
My inspiration.

Oma's twenty-first gift of advice:

No one who is successful walked alone.
Seek out teachers and willingly receive whatever they offer.

$\mathcal{S}$ome refer to them as guides, guardian angels, soul friends, teachers, helpers, heroes or masters. Whatever the case is for you, accept and receive any wisdom they want to give. Every business person out there at one point had to ask for outside confidence in terms of capital and first-time client referrals. Make a point to surround yourself with people that you admire, because one day this will allow you to meet or surpass your own expectations.

At times during Oma's life, she needed support. Various generous individuals in the community provided this support. When she first began accepting disabled children, many of their parents couldn't afford to give her any financial contributions. Oma and Opa worked very hard and depended on outside income from his labor jobs to pay for necessities for the children. Throughout this time, there were various established individuals who came to their aid by selling land at affordable prices, making donations, volunteering hours or spreading public awareness through word of mouth.

When you are truly on your path, you find the most interesting collaborations occurring even without your initiation. It is truly a great feeling to get up in the morning, energized and ready for another 12-hour day. Open your heart to accepting the road of life purpose and contribution. It is just as important to pray in the good times as in the bad. If life is satisfactory right now and you |don't want to rock the boat, what will you do when the storm crosses over and someone else rocks it for you? Learn to surf the tidal waves so that your life becomes a pipeline of adventure. Strive to never live unconsciously again. I guarantee that when you embrace this idea and incorporate it into your life, your vision will become clear and openings will begin to flow into your life from all different directions.

Oma's twenty-second gift of advice:

Watch and treasure the children in your life
for they are the bearers of unconditional love and support.

Oma surrounded herself with children and related to them at a level that sought to honor their forms of communication.

For me as a child, there was no place better than Oma's house. She knew how to talk to me in a way that confirmed her respect, and she intently listened to what I had to say. Many adults speak down or over children, or listen with closed ears when their children are sharing their opinions and ideas. Children are very smart and are the first to pick up on this sham.

Another exciting time for me was at grace around the dinner table. Being young, I still didn't comprehend why such a thing as thanks should be so serious. When the person requested to say grace began, they would say, "Close your eyes, let us pray." I would, for a split second, and then quickly open them so as to not miss anything, and to watch the phenomenon as suddenly everyone went from merriment to solemnity. But sure enough, every time, there was another pair of eyes twinkling back at me. Oma and I would share a bonding moment, looking at each other and then blinking at the "Amen" so as to trick everyone into thinking that both of us were just opening our eyes. As I grew older and other grandchildren came into the picture, I would still keep my eyes open; along the way some of the other toddlers would join in.

Another moment I remember involved preparing beans we had just picked from Opa's garden for dinner. Sitting on the porch, Oma, my sister and I entertained each other while completing what should have been a tedious task. All of a sudden, Oma sneezed and her teeth came bounding out of her mouth, landing on the bed of freshly snapped green beans. My eyes grew round and my mouth dropped in shock as I tried to imagine how teeth could remove themselves so easily from her mouth. My sister was stunned, as well, waiting in anticipation for Oma's next move. Without a blink, Oma casually placed her teeth back in her mouth, and then simply laughed and explained the "magic" of false teeth while carrying on with the beans.

Oma showed her knowledge of children by treating our curiosity with seriousness. Most other adults I remember reacted by asking me not to stare, or by telling me I would learn later in life what was now so shocking.

Oma and I never spoke of such moments, and yet they were like whispered secrets shared between two girlfriends. Through shared moments of mischievous behavior, Oma created a warm home in many hearts. Her youthful spirit and excellent state of physical and mental health belied her advancing years.

These memories led me to visit two of Oma's best girlfriends over lunch one day. I wanted to know about the Oma who let her hair down and laughed for a few brief moments while the troubles of life waited on the sidelines. Sure enough, in every second sentence these girlfriends commented on Oma's youthful spirit. But something beyond what was said drew me into the conversation. It was the much sought-after sparkle in their eyes. These two daring ladies were filled with love of life no matter what circumstances they faced. They both were full of laughter and stories.

At 91, Ethel was not your ordinary person; in fact, she was a bundle of fire—full of inspiration, positive energy and a wealth of wisdom. Ethel was brilliant and fast with every comment and movement. Her nature was kind and courteous and she drew a smile from every nearby table. Her life had had hardships as well as good moments, but she never stayed tied down. Instead she put out her wings and held on for the ride.

Hazel was also a delight to lunch with that day. Hearing the stories of Oma from her perspective helped me to understand how Oma had balanced her hectic life. Hazel, who is the same age as Oma, was born in 1914 and continues to be an extraordinary light, bringing love and joy to many in her community. Our conversation reminded me of Oma's own progressive nature and her open mind which I hope to always integrate into my own life.

On the day Holland was liberated, there was much celebration. At this time Canadian soldiers were greatly admired because of their role in Holland's release from the Nazi occupation. Accompanied by some of her friends, Oma went into the heart of her village disguised as a Canadian soldier. She had been able to convince a patient to lend her his uniform, and she drew on a fake moustache. Because many people in her village could not speak English, Oma's English was interpreted as Canadian. That night, Oma and her friends danced with many people. All of the girls swooned and bragged about dancing with a real Canadian soldier. When Oma returned home, her father told her that he didn't have any more room for anyone to stay. Oma laughed and wiped off her moustache, which shocked her unsuspecting father.

You don't need to live through such things to be able to take Oma's life as a living example to inspire your own. You can live with your blinders off and your mind expanded, open and ready to learn something new daily.

As I sat across the table admiring these two sweet courageous women, I knew without a second thought why Oma surrounded herself with Hazel and Ethel whenever the hills of life seemed too high to climb. It reminded me of Oma's advice to be careful of those with whom you surround yourself because they reflect who you aspire to be. I knew that afternoon that Oma found her home away from home with these two ladies, and that through each other's clear, purposeful spirits, each of these ladies gained strength and support. They were able to share rare moments of laughter and childish fun.

It all comes back to honoring your inner child. It is a truth that has been known by the wise for thousands of years.

What Oma, Hazel and Ethel revealed through their inspiring conversation, lives and inner natures was the long-awaited solution to an age-old problem. The secret to youth could not be swallowed, inhaled or applied with a brush. Instead, it was a constant nurturing of the soul, created by cultivating a colorful life full of family, friendship and laughter.

By the time you reach 87, it is moments—not society, rules or obligations—that govern the richness of your life. Why wait so long? Why not learn this wisdom now, and like Oma, Hazel and Ethel, live a life full of moments and memories so lively you don't have to go to the movies to be entertained!

Oma's twenty-third gift of advice:

There is sunshine in my soul today.

Oma's precious final gift was the incredible transition from life to death. It is that undiscovered partnership wherein what is of this world joins with that of the unknown.

Oma was the type of person who never shared her problems as she felt everyone had their own load to carry. She was the constant and steadfast listener guiding any lost soul through the arising fog of life's cycles. In her final year, she battled leukemia. She never seemed to miss a step and continued to host the overflow of expected and unexpected guests daily. Oma still brought gifts to the poor, visited with people she called elderly (who were decades younger), still donated when and where she could, and nursed all her children and grandchildren through what now seem to be needless sorrows.

Yet though her spirit remained strong, her body began to grow weaker. In March of 2001, Oma had a pain in her side and decided to go to the hospital. Upon seeing her condition, the hospital admitted her and placed her in palliative care. At the beginning of her hospital visit, she told everyone not to worry because on the day the snow left she would get to go home. Day and night the family sat with her, and during each one of those days another organ would give way.

Despite all of the fuss around her, Oma's eyes still shone and lit up when anyone walked in the room. Through to the final hour, Oma nursed and cared for every soul that came in to her room.

On a Tuesday, after I was finished teaching, I went to the hospital to visit Oma. My sister arrived shortly after. Together we found hymn books, and began singing Oma's favorite hymns. Throughout Oma's final years, she often spoke of wanting cheerful songs sung at her burial.

We came to the hymn "There is Sunshine in My Soul Today" and began to sing. Within a few moments, the breathing that had become laborious over the previous week became silent and normal. A peace washed over the entire room and Oma smiled.

Then with a calm ease, her hands raised up, and without a sound she slipped away with wonder and happiness emanating from her eyes. In that moment, I understood that death is not a finality but a new beginning. There is no fight when you meet death with the security of having lived a life of radiant contribution. As I left the hospital that night, I couldn't help but notice the warm breeze. I realized that day had been the first day without snow. As she predicted, Oma had gone home.

The words of the hymn still echo in my head: *There is springtime in my soul today, for when the lord is near. The dove of peace sings in my heart, the flowers of grace appear.* Truly in those final moments, Oma experienced a rebirth into a new spring that was filled with peace.

I cannot express how blessed I feel to have been given the honor of experiencing something so rare and yet so real—the gift of knowledge that there is peace and joy on the other side of life as we know it. How you name heaven doesn't matter so much as the acknowledgement of a journey after death, that in the final moments of a life well lived, there is acceptance and joy.

After you read the final pages of this book, keep the wisdom of Oma alive within you. Know that you have the potential, talent and character to be incredible, because you already are. Take with you throughout your day the wisdom of knowing who you are and the strength to live your legacy. Allow those who come into contact with you daily to experience the wonder of who you are. Help those in need, without allowing their issues to dampen your light. Remember that in all the darkness lurking in the world, no light can be too bright. Never downplay the talent that you encase. As ideas begin to flow through your mind, remember you have many possibilities awaiting you. You don't have to follow them all right away. Take time out to enjoy your successes.

Let Oma's legacy be a support and guide for you to start living your own. Find jungles to travel in, stereotypes to break and causes to fight for. Create laugh lines and compose a physical map of the joy you emulate.

Thank you for sharing this journey with us. I give thanks for the interconnected links of life and know that you were meant to cross my path, as I yours.

Have a great life!

With much love and blessings,

Karen Vos Braun

There Is Sunshine in My Soul Today.

Text: Eliza E. Hewitt   Music: John R. Sweney

There is Sunshine in my soul today,
More Glorious and bright
Than glows in any earthly sky,
For Jesus is my light.

O there's sunshine, blessed sunshine,
when the peaceful happy moments roll;
when Jesus shows his smiling face,
There is sunshine in my soul.

There is music in my soul today,
A carol to my king.
And Jesus listening can hear,
The songs I cannot sing.

There is springtime in my soul today,
For when the lord is near
The dove of peace sings in my heart,
The flowers of grace appear.

There is gladness in my soul today,
And hope and love and praise
For blessings which he gives me now,
For joys in future days.

O there's sunshine, blessed sunshine,
when the peaceful happy moments roll;
when Jesus shows his smiling face,
There is sunshine in my soul.

Afterword—The Life of Johanna Vos

While this book was in progress, many readers had questions about Oma's life and wanted more information. The following is by no means a biography, but more a chronological collection of some of the tales I heard from Oma.

On May 28, 1914, in the village of Witmarsum Friesland, Johanna Stoffels was born in a windmill, the youngest of eleven children. As a young girl, one of Johanna's favorite pastimes was visiting with people who were sick. By bringing them flowers or treats, Johanna enjoyed lighting up their lives.

At the age of 17, Johanna was inspired to create a life mission statement, which was to help those who could not help themselves. Johanna knew at a young age that "when you have an open heart and are on a clear path, openings come into your life from all different directions."

Johanna began her nursing training in 1936 in a hospital that had only fifteen nurses. It was at this hospital that Johanna would learn the skills she would need later in her life.

In 1940, Johanna moved to an academic hospital in Groningen. On her first day of work, World

War II broke out in Holland. She was asked to cover all the hospital windows with black paper and move the patients to the basement. All the young mothers on the maternity floor were sent home to their villages with their babies. The newborns were bundled in baskets with identification labels attached should anything happen.

One night, Johanna awoke thinking the moon was particularly bright. She soon realized the city was being bombed, and she rushed to the hospital in anticipation of the arrival of wounded civilians.

Johanna remained a nurse at the academic hospital throughout the Nazi occupation of Holland. Groningen was the closest hospital to the concentration camp of Westerborg. Patients would often be brought in from the camp suffering from various ailments. Johanna and the other nurses would lie to the Nazi soldiers and try to keep the patients in the hospital for as long as possible. It was not unusual to see patients arriving at the hospital at less than half their normal weight.

Johanna was part of an underground operation that hid Jewish people from the Nazis. She enlisted her sister's help and hid three people under the floor in secret rooms in her home. As a nurse, she assisted in the escape of many patients from the hospital. It was a miracle that Johanna herself was not caught by the Nazi party, as her grandmother had been Jewish.

Johanna became a Victorian Order Nurse (VON) during what was to be the last year of the war. Thereafter, she accepted a position in Suriname in the jungle, where she set up the first medical clinic in the area.

Johanna loved her work there. She would travel the rivers throughout the jungle by boat and deliver supplies to those in need. She struggled daily between the world of tribal medicine and western medicine, and learned to appreciate the value of both. It was during her years in the jungle that Johanna met her future husband, a missionary who was assisting tribes with agriculture.

Johanna married Pieter Vos on June 12, 1948, and together they worked in the poor districts of Suriname. Unfortunately over time, Johanna became very sick with malaria and had to return to the city, to Paramaribo.

Soon Johanna's first baby was born and would be the eldest of six children. Johanna and Pieter moved back to Holland with their young family and applied for a sponsorship to Canada.

A family in Linwood, Ontario, accepted the sponsorship and the Vos family moved to Linwood. Not long after, they moved off the farm to Kitchener, Ontario, where they purchased their first home. Johanna took borders into the house and Pieter held three jobs that paid 80 cents an hour in order to create a firm foundation for their family. It was during this busy time that Corrie Ten Boom came to Canada and visited Johanna and Pieter in their home.

One night after reading in the paper about the need for care in the area of mentally and physically challenged children, Johanna and Pieter immediately felt that they had found their unique calling. They contacted the authors of the article, and Johanna went and stayed with them for a few weeks to learn as much as she could about caring for these children. It was not long before the rooms of their home were turned into spaces for children.

Johanna had to be resourceful in terms of finding beds and clothing for all the children in need, and as time passed, it was clear that expanded facilities were required. Thus the Sunbeam Home was born. The name Sunbeam Home came from the children's hymn "I Want to Be a Sunbeam for Jesus."

Within a short time, the community responded to the couple's efforts and began helping in various ways. This outpouring of support confirmed to Johanna and Pieter that they had indeed found their true path. Johanna devoted her time to the Sunbeam Home until she retired.

Johanna passed away with leukemia on March 20, 2001, while family members at her bedside sang the hymn "There Is Sunshine in My Soul Today."

We hope you have enjoyed reading *The Wisdom of Oma*.

If you would like to order additional copies, please visit innervoice.ca on the Internet.

You may also order by sending a cheque
or money order to:

Inner Voice
5-420 Erb Street W., Suite 434
Waterloo ON N2L 6K6

Name: _____

Address: _____

_____

_____ Postal Code _____

Telephone Number: _____

Your book(s) will be sent by post.
Please allow 2 – 3 weeks for delivery.

INNER *Voice*

5-420 Erb Street W.
Suite 434
Waterloo ON
N2L 6K6
(519) 502-6047
www.innervoice.ca

Number of copies _____
@ $16.95 CDN or 12.95 USD = $ _____

Add GST @ 7%
(Canadian residents only)   = $ _____

Add shipping and handling:
$4.00 for one book +
$1.00 for each additional
book to a maximum of $10.00 = $ _____

Total = $ _____

(US orders, please submit in US funds)

VISA or Mastercard orders are also accepted.

Card number _____

Exp. date: _____

Signature _____